STEP-BY-STEP
Low Fat Cookbook

STEP-BY-STEP
Low Fat Cookbook

Catherine Atkinson

Photographs by James Duncan

LORENZ BOOKS

This edition published in 1998 by Lorenz Books

© Anness Publishing Limited 1995

Lorenz Books is an imprint of
Anness Publishing Limited
Hermes House, 88-89 Blackfriars Road
London SE1 8HA

ISBN 1 85967 716 9 (paperback)

A CIP catalogue record for this book
is available from the British Library

Publisher: Joanna Lorenz
Series Editor: Lindsay Porter
Designer: Peter Laws
Photographer: James Duncan
Stylist: Madeleine Brehaut

Printed and bound in Hong Kong

1 3 5 7 9 10 8 6 4 2

MEASUREMENTS
Three sets of measurements have been provided here, in the following order:
Metric, Imperial and American. It is essential that units of measurement are not mixed
within each recipe. Where conversions result in awkward numbers, these have been
rounded for convenience, but are still accurate enough to produce successful results.

CONTENTS

INTRODUCTION

So much has been written in the past decade about what we should and shouldn't eat, it's hardly surprising we're sceptical about dietary advice – it seems that everything we enjoy is bad for us. Often nutritionists are vague and simply suggest eating 'a balanced diet'. However, when it comes to avoiding heart disease, recommendations are loud and clear: reduce your intake of fat (especially saturated) and you'll considerably reduce the risk of heart disease.

But what does this mean when you're shopping at the supermarket, faced with confusingly labelled foods? What exactly is saturated fat and how do we begin to limit the amount of fat we eat? These are the questions that are answered in this book.

Cutting down on fat doesn't mean sacrificing taste. It's easy to follow a healthy eating plan without becoming a faddist. There's no need to forgo all your favourite foods, as the recipes in this book illustrate, but you may have to alter your approach to cooking and choose ingredients that are naturally lower in fat and prepare them with little – if any – additional fat. This is not as limiting as it sounds – you can still enjoy hearty main courses and desserts so delicious it's hard to believe they're good for you. With this in mind, it won't be long before you develop a preference for lower fat versions of everyday foods.

Facts about Fats

It's important to know something about different fats before we can make changes to the way we eat – some fats are believed to be less harmful than others.

Fats in our foods are made up of building blocks of fatty acids and glycerol and their properties vary according to each combination. There are three main types of fatty acids; saturated, polyunsaturated and unsaturated or mono-unsaturated. There is always a combination of each of the three types in any food, but the amount of each type varies greatly from one food to another.

SATURATED FATS

All fatty acids are made up of chains of carbon atoms. Each atom has one or more free 'bonds' to link with other atoms and by doing so the fatty acid transports nutrients to cells throughout the body. Without these free 'bonds' the atom cannot form any links, that is to say, it's completely 'saturated'. Because of this, the body finds it hard to process the fatty acid into energy, so simply stores it as fat.

The main type of saturated fat is found in food of animal origin – meat and dairy products such as lard and butter, which are solid at room temperature. However, there are also some saturated fats of vegetable origin, notably coconut and palm oils. A few margarines and oils are processed by changing some of the unsaturated fatty acids to saturated ones; these are labelled 'hydrogenated vegetable oil' and should be avoided.

MONO-UNSATURATED FATS

These are found in foods such as olive oil, rapeseed oil, some nuts, oily fish and avocado pears. They may help lower the blood cholesterol and this could explain why in Mediterranean countries there is such a low incidence of heart disease.

Above: *Some oils, such as olive and rapeseed are thought to help lower blood cholesterol.*

Above left: *Animal products such as lard and butter and some margarines are major sources of saturated fats.*

POLYUNSATURATED FATS

There are two types, those of vegetable or plant origin, such as sunflower oil, soft margarine and seeds (omega 6) and those from oily fish (omega 3). Both are usually liquid at room temperature.

At one time it was believed to be beneficial to switch to polyunsaturates as they may also help lower cholesterol. Today most experts believe that it's more important to reduce the total intake of all kinds of fat.

Right: *Vegetable and plant oils and some margarines are high in polyunsaturated fat.*

The Cholesterol Question

Cholesterol is a fat-like substance which plays a vital role in the body. It's the material from which many essential hormones and vitamin D are made. However, too much saturated fat encourages the body to make more cholesterol than it needs or can get rid of.

Cholesterol is carried around the body, attached to proteins called high density lipoproteins (HDL), low density lipoproteins (LDL), and very low density lipoproteins (VLDL or triglycerides). After eating, the LDLs carry the fat in the blood to the cells where it's required. Any surplus should be excreted from the body; however, if there is too much LDL in the blood, some of the fat will be deposited on the walls of the arteries. This furring up gradually narrows the arteries and is one of the most common causes of heart attacks and strokes. In contrast, HDLs appear to protect against heart disease. Whether high triglyceride levels are risk factors remains unknown.

For some people, an excess of cholesterol in the blood is a hereditary trait; in others, it's mainly due to the consumption of too much saturated fat. In both cases though, it can be reduced by a low fat diet. Many people believe naturally high cholesterol foods such as egg yolks and offal should be avoided, but research has shown that it is more important to reduce total fat intake.

FATS & OILS		
Saturated	**Mono-unsaturated**	**Polyunsaturated**
Butter	Olive oil	Corn oil
Lard	Grapeseed oil	Safflower oil
Hard margarine	Rapeseed oil	Soya oil
Suet		Sunflower oil
Vegetarian suet		Walnut oil
Coconut oil		Soft margarines, labelled 'high in polyunsaturates'
Palm oil		

Planning a Low Fat Diet

Most of us eat about 115 g/4 oz of fat everyday. Yet just 10 g/¼ oz – that's about the amount in a single packet of crisps or a thin slice of Cheddar cheese – is all we actually need.

Current nutritional advice isn't quite that strict though and suggests that we should limit our daily intake to no more than 30% of total calories. In real terms, this means that for an average intake of 2000 calories a day, 30% of energy would come from 600 calories. Since each gram of fat provides 9 calories, your total daily intake should be no more than 66.6 g fat. If you look at page 11 you'll see how easy it is to consume this amount and how you can cut down.

It's easy to cut down on obvious sources of fat such as butter, margarine, cream, whole milk and high fat cheeses, but watch out for 'hidden' fats in food. We tend to think of cakes and biscuits as 'sweet' foods, but usually more calories come from their fat content than from the sugar. Fat makes up about half the weight of nuts and even the leanest red meat, completely trimmed of all visible fat, still contains about 10% fat. About one-quarter of the fat we eat comes from meat and meat products, one-fifth from dairy products and margarine and the rest from cakes, biscuits, pastries and other foods.

Butter vs Margarine

Butter and margarine producers have spent thousands on advertising, trying to convince us that their product is the healthiest. Both butter and margarine contain 80% fat and the same number of calories (737 Kcals/3087 kJ in 100 g/3½ oz). Butter, however in saturated fat. Margarine may also contain a high proportion of saturated fat, or it may be a type that is high in polyunsaturates, so it's important to check the label.

Low fat spreads and half fat or reduced fat butters contain 40% fat; the rest is water and milk solids emulsified together. There are also 'very low fat' spreads around, containing 20–30% fat. Some are less palatable than others, so it's worth trying several to find one you like the taste of!

Labelling

Look at labels when choosing food. Ingredients are listed in order of quantity, so watch out for those with fat near the top. Nutritional labels can be misleading if you don't understand what they mean.

Low fat
Contains less than half the fat of the standard product. Remember that some foods are very high in fat. Think twice about buying 'low fat' sausages or crisps.

Reduced fat
Contains less than 75% of the fat of the standard product.

Low cholesterol
No more than 0.005% of the total fat is cholesterol.

High in polyunsaturates/low in saturates
Contains at least 35% fat of which at least 45% of the fatty acids are polyunsaturated and not more than 25% saturated.

The Lowdown on Low Fat

Reduce your fat intake simply by switching to lower fat foods.

0.2 g fat
5 ml/1 tsp whole milk
200 ml/7 fl oz/scant 1 cup skimmed milk

1.0 g fat
115 g/4 oz/½ cup low fat natural yogurt
15 g/½ oz Greek yogurt
1 thin slice (1/20) avocado pear
3 bananas
9 apples, apricots, peaches, pears,
oranges or small bunches of grapes

2.5 g fat
¼ back bacon rasher
8 turkey rashers

10 g/¼ oz fat
115 g/4 oz/½ cup fat reduced cocoa powder
50 g/2 oz/¼ cup cocoa powder

12 g fat
15 g/½ oz butter
25 g/1 oz low fat spread

15 g/½ oz fat
50 g/2 oz Cheddar cheese
65 g/2½ oz Edam cheese
75 g/3 oz feta cheese
100 g/4 oz fat reduced cheddar
200 g/7 oz cottage cheese

WEIGHING NOTE
The weights given here have been
rounded slightly up or down to make
measuring portions easier.

Choosing Foods

The amount of fat, particularly saturated fat, is affected by two main factors – the type of foods we eat most often and the way in which we prepare and cook them.

Low fat doesn't mean no fat. It's misleading to start thinking simply of 'good' and 'bad' foods, it's really how much we eat of them that matters.

If you are going to cut down your fat intake, you'll need to make other alterations to your diet to compensate. High-fibre fruit, vegetables and cereals will help fill the gap. You should aim to increase your intake of carbohydrate foods to provide more than half your energy requirements. This will not only make your diet healthier, but you will also gradually lose weight, should you need to do this.

cheese'. By definition, a low fat soft cheese must contain no more than 10% milk fat, although many are fat free. Medium fat soft cheese has 10–20% milk fat. By comparison, cream cheese has more than 45% milk fat, so a switch to any of the others is a good move.

MEAT AND FISH
Always trim meat of any visible fat and skim stocks and casseroles (this is easiest if you cool them first). Buy back bacon rather than streaky bacon and cut all the fat off before cooking. The red meats –

lamb, pork and beef – are the highest in saturated fats, so try to eat chicken and turkey more often, but always remove the skin, which is high in fat. Avoid meat products such as sausages, salami and pâtés which are very high in fat.

Fish has a lower fat content than meat, and fish oils may help reduce blood cholesterol levels, although this remains unproven. Certainly, fish oils make blood clotting less likely to occur and as clots are an important factor in causing heart attacks, consumption of fish may be beneficial.

MILK, YOGURT AND CREAM
The fat content of ordinary milk is not particularly high – 3.9 g per 100 g of milk – but you may consume quite a lot in tea, coffee or cooking. If you drink a pint of milk a day, you'll be adding about 20 g of fat to your intake. It's therefore worth switching to skimmed milk, which has virtually all the fat content removed, or at least to semi-skimmed milk. Beware of dried skimmed milk and coffee creamers – these may be skimmed of animal fat, but may have vegetable fat added.

Yogurt allows low fat foodies to enjoy many dishes that would otherwise be denied to them because of their cream content. Low fat natural yogurt has less than 2% fat, but if you need a thicker product for cooking, strain off some of the whey (see page 21), or use Greek strained yogurt. It contains 9–10% fat, but as double cream contains about 48% fat, it's still a good choice.

Half fat versions of single, double and whipping creams are also available; but don't be too lavish with them as they're still fairly high in fat.

CHEESE
One-third of hard cheese is fat. Even Continental cheeses such as Edam contain about one-fifth fat. It is, however, a useful flavouring ingredient in cooking if used sparingly. Choose a strongly-flavoured cheese like mature Cheddar or Parmesan and you'll need a lot less. There are also reduced fat alternatives to Cheddar and Cheshire which contain about half the fat of their full fat counterparts. These are good for 'eating', but are less successful for cooking.

Low fat soft or curd cheese is an excellent substitute for cream cheese. Look out too for 'quark' and various cheeses which may be simply labelled as 'skimmed milk soft cheese' or 'half fat creamery

Easy Ways to Cut Down Fat and Saturated Fat

EAT LESS	**TRY INSTEAD**
Butter and hard fats.	Try spreading butter more thinly, or replace it with a low fat spread or polyunsaturated margarine.
Fatty meats and high fat products such as pies and sausages.	Buy the leanest cuts of meat you can afford and choose low fat meats like skinless chicken or turkey. Look for reduced fat sausages and meat products. Eat fish more often, especially oily fish.
Full fat dairy products like cream, butter, hard margarine, milk and hard cheeses.	Choose skimmed or semi-skimmed milk and milk products, and try low fat yogurt, low fat fromage frais and lower fat cheeses such as skimmed milk soft cheese, reduced fat Cheddar, mozzarella or Brie.
Hard cooking fats such as lard or hard margarine.	Choose mono-unsaturated or polyunsaturated oils for cooking, such as olive, sunflower, corn or soya oil.
Rich salad dressings like mayonnaise or salad cream.	Make salad dressings with low fat yogurt or fromage frais, or use a healthy oil such as olive oil.
Fried foods.	Grill, microwave, steam or bake when possible. Roast meats on a rack. Fill up on starchy foods like pasta, rice and couscous. Choose jacket or boiled potatoes, not chips.
Added fat in cooking.	Use heavy-based or non-stick pans so you can cook with little or no added fat.
High fat snacks such as crisps, chocolate, cakes, pastries and biscuits.	Choose fresh or dried fruit, breadsticks or vegetable sticks. Make your own low fat cakes and bakes.

The Fat and Calorie Contents of Food

The following figures show the weight of fat (g) and the energy content of 115 g/4 oz of each food.

VEGETABLES	Fat (g)	Energy
Broccoli	0.9	33 Kcals/1380 kJ
Cabbage	0.4	26 Kcals/109 kJ
Cauliflower	0.9	34 Kcals/142 kJ
Carrots	0.3	35 Kcals/146 kJ
Courgettes	0.4	18 Kcals/75 kJ
Cucumber	0.1	10 Kcals/42 kJ
Mushrooms	0.5	13 Kcals/54 kJ
Onions	0.2	36 Kcals/151 kJ
Peas	1.5	83 Kcals/347 kJ
Potatoes	0.2	75 Kcals/314 kJ
Chips, homemade	6.7	189 Kcals/791 kJ
Chips, retail	12.4	239 Kcals/1000 kJ
Oven-chips, frozen, baked	4.2	163 Kcals/682 kJ
Tomatoes	0.3	17 Kcals/71 kJ
Chick-peas, whole, dried	5.4	320 Kcals/1339 kJ
Hummus	12.6	187 Kcals/782 kJ
Red kidney beans, dried	1.1	279 Kcals/1167 kJ

Information from **The Composition of Foods**, 5th Edition, (1991) is reproduced with the permission of the Royal Society of Chemistry and the Controller of Her Majesty's Stationery Office.

FISH	Fat (g)	Energy
Cod fillets, raw	0.7	76 Kcals/317 kJ
Cod in batter, fried in oil	10.3	199 Kcals/833 kJ
Crab, canned	0.9	81 Kcals/339 kJ
Haddock, raw	0.6	73 Kcals/305 kJ
Lemon sole, raw	1.4	81 Kcals/339 kJ
Prawns	1.8	107 Kcals/448 kJ
Trout, steamed	4.5	135 Kcals/565 kJ

MEAT PRODUCTS	Fat (g)	Energy
Bacon rasher, streaky	39.5	414 Kcals/1732 kJ
Turkey rasher	1.0	99 Kcals/414 kJ
Beef mince, raw	16.2	221 Kcals/925 kJ
Rump steak, lean and fat	12.1	218 Kcals/912 kJ
Rump steak, lean only	6.0	168 Kcals/703 kJ
Lamp chops, loin, lean and fat	29.0	355 Kcals/1485 kJ
Lamb chops, loin, lean only	12.3	122 Kcals/928 kJ
Pork chops, loin, lean and fat	24.2	332 Kcals/1390 kJ
Pork chops, loin, lean only	10.7	226 Kcals/945 kJ
Chicken fillet, raw	2.7	109 Kcals/456 kJ
Chicken fillet, breaded, fried oil	12.7	242 Kcals/1012 kJ
Duck, meat only, raw	4.8	122 Kcals/510 kJ
Duck, roasted, meat, fat and skin	29.0	339 Kcals/1418 kJ
Turkey, meat only, raw	2.2	107 Kcals/448 kJ
Liver, lamb, raw	10.3	179 Kcals/749 kJ
Pork pie	27.0	376 Kcals/1573 kJ
Salami	45.2	491 Kcals/2054 kJ

DAIRY, FATS & OILS	Fat (g)	Energy
Cream, double	48.0	449 Kcals/1897 kJ
Cream, single	19.1	198 Kcals/828 kJ
Cream, whipping	39.3	373 Kcals/1560 kJ
Milk, skimmed	0.1	33 Kcals/130 kJ
Milk, whole	3.9	66 Kcals/276 kJ
Brie	26.9	319 Kcals/1335 kJ
Cheddar cheese	34.4	412 Kcals/1724 kJ
Cheddar-type, reduced fat	15.0	261 Kcals/1092 kJ
Cream cheese	47.4	439 Kcals/1837 kJ
Edam cheese	25.4	333 Kcals/1393 kJ
Feta cheese	20.2	250 Kcals/1046 kJ
Parmesan cheese	32.7	452 Kcals/1891 kJ
Low fat yogurt, plain	0.8	56 Kcals/234 kJ
Greek yogurt	9.1	115 Kcals/481 kJ
Butter	81.7	737 Kcals/308 kJ
Margarine	81.6	739 Kcals/3092 kJ
Low fat spread	40.5	390 Kcals/1632 kJ
Lard	99.0	891 Kcals/3730 kJ
Coconut oil	99.9	899 Kcals/3761 kJ
Corn oil	99.9	899 Kcals/3761 kJ
Olive oil	99.9	899 Kcals/3761 kJ
Safflower oil	99.9	899 Kcals/3761 kJ
Eggs (about 2, size 4)	10.9	147 Kcals/615 kJ
Egg yolk	30.5	339 Kcals/1418 kJ
Egg white	Trace	36 Kcals/150 kJ

CEREALS, BAKING & PRESERVES	Fat (g)	Energy
Brown rice, uncooked	2.8	357 Kcals/1494 kJ
White rice, uncooked	3.6	383 Kcals/1602 kJ
Pasta, white, uncooked	1.8	342 Kcals/1431 kJ
Brown bread	2.0	218 Kcals/912 kJ
Croissant	20.3	360 Kcals/1506 kJ
Flapjack	26.6	484 Kcals/2025 kJ
Shortbread	26.1	498 Kcals/2084 kJ
Digestive biscuit (plain)	20.9	471 Kcals/1971 kJ
Madeira cake	16.9	393 Kcals/1644 kJ
Fatless sponge cake	6.1	294 Kcals/1230 kJ
Sugar, white	0	394 Kcals/1648 kJ
Chocolate, milk	30.3	529 Kcals/2213 kJ
Honey	0	288 Kcals/1205 kJ
Lemon Curd	5.1	283 Kcals/1184 kJ
Fruit jam	0	261 Kcals/1092 kJ
Marmalade	0	261 Kcals/1092 kJ

FRUIT & NUTS	Fat (g)	Energy
Apples, eating	0.1	47 Kcals/197 kJ
Avocados	19.5	190 Kcals/795 kJ
Bananas	0.3	95 Kcals/397 kJ
Dried mixed fruit	1.6	227 Kcals/950 kJ
Grapefruit	0.1	30 Kcals/125 kJ
Oranges	0.1	37 Kcals/155 kJ
Peaches	0.1	33 Kcals/138 kJ
Almonds	55.8	612 Kcals/2560 kJ
Brazil nuts	68.2	682 Kcals/2853 kJ
Pine nuts	68.6	688 Kcals/2878 kJ
Peanut butter, smooth	53.7	623 Kcals/2606 kJ

Equipment

There are only a few essentials for low fat recipes – accurate measuring and weighing equipment and a non-stick frying pan. There are, however, many gadgets which make cooking with the minimum of fat a lot easier.

non-stick baking paper

non-stick baking tins

Baking sheet
A flat, rigid, non-stick baking sheet ensures even cooking.

Baking tray
A shallow-sided non-stick tray that won't buckle at high temperatures is ideal for roasting.

Bowls
A set of bowls is useful for mixing, whisking and soaking. A non-porous material such as glass or stainless steel is essential when whisking egg whites.

Chopping board
A hygienic nylon board is recommended for chopping and cutting.

Colander
This is useful for draining cooked pasta and vegetables quickly.

Cook's knife
A large all-purpose cook's knife is essential for chopping, dicing and slicing.

Filleting knife
A thin, flexible-bladed knife is useful for filleting fish.

Frying pan
A non-stick surface is vital for 'frying' and browning meat and vegetables.

Large spoon
Use this for folding in, stirring and basting.

Measuring cups or weighing scales
Use these for accurately measuring both dry and wet ingredients.

Measuring spoons
Essential for measuring small quantities accurately.

Non-stick coated fabric sheet
This re-usable non-stick material can be cut to size, and used to line cake tins, baking sheets or frying pans. Heat resistant up to 290°C/550°F and microwave-safe, it will last up to 5 years.

Non-stick baking paper
Ideal for lining cake tins and baking sheets without the need for greasing.

Non-stick baking tins
For easy removal of low fat bakes and sponge cakes.

Perforated spoon
Useful for lifting cooked food out of cooking liquid.

Ridged grill pan
For giving grilled meat and vegetables characteristic 'char lines'.

Sieve
For sifting dry ingredients and draining yogurt.

Small grater
For finely grating fresh Parmesan cheese and nutmeg.

Vegetable peeler
For preparing fruit and vegetables.

Whisk
Essential for whisking egg whites and for thorough mixing.

ridged grill pan

non-stick baking tins

non-stick coated fabric sheet

sieve

large spoon

baking sheet

measuring cups

chopping boards

vegetable peeler

Chicken Stock

This classic, flavourful stock forms the base for many soups and sauces.

Makes 1.5 litres/2¹/₂ pints/6¹/₄ cups

INGREDIENTS
1 kg/2¹/₄ lb chicken wings or thighs
1 onion
2 whole cloves
1 bay leaf
1 sprig of thyme
3–4 sprigs of parsley
10 black peppercorns

1 Cut the chicken into pieces and put into a large, heavy-based saucepan. Peel the onion and stick with the cloves. Tie the bay leaf, thyme, parsley and peppercorns in a piece of muslin and add to the saucepan together with the onion.

2 Pour in 1.75 litres/3 pints/7¹/₂ cups of cold water. Slowly bring to simmering point, skimming off any scum which rises to the surface with a slotted spoon. Continue to simmer very gently, uncovered, for 1¹/₂ hours.

3 Strain the stock through a sieve into a large bowl and leave until cold. Remove any fat from the surface with a slotted spoon. Keep chilled in the refrigerator until required, or freeze in usable amounts.

Vegetable Stock

A vegetarian version of the basic stock.

Makes 1.5 litres/2¹/₂ pints/6¹/₄ cups

INGREDIENTS
2 carrots
2 celery sticks
2 onions
2 tomatoes
10 mushroom stalks
2 bay leaves
1 sprig of thyme
3–4 sprigs of parsley
10 black peppercorns

1 Roughly chop the carrots, celery, onions, tomatoes and mushroom stalks. Place them in a large heavy-based saucepan. Tie the bay leaves, thyme, parsley and peppercorns in a piece of muslin and add to the pan.

2 Pour in 1.75 litres/3 pints/7¹/₂ cups cold water. Slowly bring to simmering point. Continue to simmer very gently, uncovered, for 1¹/₂ hours.

3 Strain through a sieve into a large bowl and leave until cold. Keep chilled in the refrigerator until required, or freeze in usable amounts.

Peeling and Seeding Tomatoes

This is an efficient way of preparing tomatoes.

1 Use a sharp knife to cut a small cross on the bottom of the tomato.

2 Turn the tomato over and cut out the core.

3 Immerse the tomato in boiling water for 10–15 seconds, then transfer to a bowl of cold water using a slotted spoon.

4 Lift out the tomato and peel (the skin should be easy to remove).

5 Cut the tomato in half crosswise and squeeze out the seeds.

6 Use a large knife to cut the peeled tomato into strips, then chop across the strips to make dice.

Sautéed Onions

Fried onions form the basis of many savoury recipes. This is a fat free version.

INGREDIENTS
2 medium onions, sliced
175 ml/6 fl oz/¾ cup chicken or
 vegetable stock
15 ml/1 tbsp dry red or white wine or
 wine vinegar

1 Put the onions and stock into a non-stick frying pan. Cover and bring to the boil. Simmer for 1 minute.

2 Uncover and boil for about 5 minutes, or until the stock has reduced entirely. Lower the heat and stir the onions until just beginning to colour.

3 Add the wine or vinegar and continue to cook until the onions are dry and lightly browned.

Whipped 'Cream'

Serve this sweet 'cream' instead of whipped double cream. It isn't suitable for cooking, but freezes very well.

Makes 150 ml/¼ pint/⅔ cup

INGREDIENTS
2.5 ml/½ tsp powdered gelatine
50 g/2 oz/¼ cup skimmed milk
 powder
15 ml/1 tbsp caster sugar
15 ml/1 tbsp lemon juice

1 Sprinkle the gelatine over 15 ml/1 tbsp cold water in a small bowl and leave to 'sponge' for 5 minutes. Place the bowl over a saucepan of hot water and stir until dissolved. Leave to cool.

2 Whisk the skimmed milk powder, caster sugar, lemon juice and 60 ml/4 tbsp cold water until frothy. Add the dissolved gelatine and whisk for a few seconds more. Chill in the refrigerator for 30 minutes.

3 Whisk the chilled mixture again until very thick and frothy. Serve within 30 minutes of making.

Strained Yogurt and Simple Curd Cheese

Strained yogurt and curd cheese are simple to make at home, and tend to be lower in fat than commercial varieties. Serve strained yogurt with puddings instead of cream, sweetened with a little honey, if liked. Curd cheese can be used instead of soured cream, cream cheese or butter, flavoured with chopped herbs.

Makes 300 ml/¹/₂ pint/1¹/₄ cups strained yogurt or

115 g/4 oz/¹/₂ cup curd cheese

INGREDIENTS
600 ml/1 pint/2¹/₂ cups natural low fat
   yogurt

1 Line a nylon or stainless steel sieve with a double layer of muslin. Put over a bowl and pour in the yogurt.

2 Leave to drain in the refrigerator for 3 hours – it will have separated into thick strained yogurt and watery whey.

3 For curd cheese, leave to drain in the refrigerator for 8 hours or overnight. Spoon the curd cheese into a bowl, cover and keep chilled until required.

Yogurt Piping Cream

This is an excellent alternative to whipped cream for decorating cakes and desserts.

Makes 450 ml/³/₄ pint/scant 2 cups

INGREDIENTS
10 ml/2 tsp powdered gelatine
300 ml/¹/₂ pint/1¹/₄ cups strained
   yogurt
15 ml/1 tbsp fructose
2.5 ml/¹/₂ tsp vanilla essence
1 egg white

1 Sprinkle the gelatine over 45 ml/3 tbsp cold water in a small bowl and leave to 'sponge' for 5 minutes. Place the bowl over a saucepan of hot water and stir until dissolved. Leave to cool.

2 Mix together the yogurt, fructose and vanilla essence. Stir in the gelatine. Chill in the refrigerator for 30 minutes, or until just beginning to set around the edges.

3 Whisk the egg white until stiff and carefully fold it into the yogurt mixture. Spoon into a piping bag fitted with a piping nozzle and use immediately.

Roasted Pepper Soup

Grilling intensifies the flavour of sweet red and yellow peppers and helps this soup keep its stunning colour.

Serves 4

INGREDIENTS
3 red peppers
1 yellow pepper
1 medium onion, chopped
1 garlic clove, crushed
750 ml/1¼ pints/3⅔ cups
    vegetable stock
15 ml/1 tbsp plain flour
salt and freshly ground black pepper
red and yellow peppers, diced,
    to garnish

peppers

flour

stock

onion

NUTRITIONAL NOTES
PER PORTION:

ENERGY 66 Kcals/277 KJ **PROTEIN** 2.26 g
FAT 0.72 g **SATURATED FAT** 0
CARBOHYDRATE 13.40 g **FIBRE** 2.54 g
ADDED SUGAR 0 **SALT** 0.01 g

1 Pre-heat the grill. Halve the peppers and cut out their stalks and white pith. Scrape out the seeds.

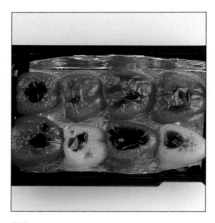

2 Line a grill pan with foil and arrange the halved peppers, skin-side up in a single layer. Grill until the skins have blackened and blistered.

3 Transfer the peppers to a plastic bag and leave until cool, then peel away their skins and discard. Roughly chop the pepper flesh.

4 Put the onion, garlic clove and 150 ml/¼ pint/⅔ cup stock into a large saucepan. Boil for about 5 minutes until most of the stock has reduced in volume. Reduce the heat and stir until softened and just beginning to colour.

5 Sprinkle the flour over the onions, then gradually stir in the remaining stock. Add the chopped, roasted peppers and bring to the boil. Cover and simmer for a further 5 minutes.

6 Leave to cool slightly, then purée in a food processor or blender until smooth. Season to taste. Return to the saucepan and re-heat until piping hot. Ladle into four soup bowls and garnish each with a sprinkling of diced peppers.

Italian Vegetable Soup

The success of this clear soup depends on the quality of the stock, so use home-made vegetable stock rather than stock cubes.

Serves 4

INGREDIENTS
1 small carrot
1 baby leek
1 celery stick
50 g/2 oz green cabbage
900 ml/1½ pints/3¾ cups
    vegetable stock
1 bay leaf
115 g/4 oz/1 cup cooked cannellini
    beans
25 g/1 oz/⅕ cup soup pasta, such as
    tiny shells, bows, stars or elbows
salt and freshly ground black pepper
snipped fresh chives, to garnish

1 Cut the carrot, leek and celery into 5 cm/2 in long julienne strips. Slice the cabbage very finely.

2 Put the stock and bay leaf into a large saucepan and bring to the boil. Add the carrot, leek and celery, cover and simmer for 6 minutes.

stock

cabbage

bay leaf

chives

baby leek

celery

carrot

pasta

NUTRITIONAL NOTES
PER PORTION:

ENERGY 69 Kcals/288 KJ **PROTEIN** 3.67 g
FAT 0.71 g **SATURATED FAT** 0.05 g
CARBOHYDRATE 12.68 g **FIBRE** 2.82 g
ADDED SUGAR 0.05 g **SALT** 0.04 g

3 Add the cabbage, beans and pasta shapes. Stir, then simmer uncovered for a further 4-5 minutes, or until the vegetables and pasta are tender.

4 Remove the bay leaf and season to taste. Ladle into four soup bowls and garnish with snipped chives. Serve immediately.

Minted Melon and Grapefruit Cocktail

Melon is always a popular starter. Here the flavour is complemented by the refreshing taste of citrus fruit and a simple dressing.

Serves 4

INGREDIENTS
1 small Galia melon, weighing about
   1 kg/2¼ lb
2 pink grapefruits
1 yellow grapefruit
5 ml/1 tsp Dijon mustard
5 ml/1 tsp raspberry or sherry vinegar
5 ml/1 tsp clear honey
15 ml/1 tbsp chopped fresh mint
sprigs of fresh mint, to garnish

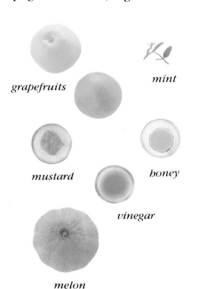

grapefruits   *mint*

mustard   *honey*

vinegar

melon

NUTRITIONAL NOTES
PER PORTION:

ENERGY 97 Kcals / 409 KJ **PROTEIN** 2.22 g
FAT 0.63 g **SATURATED FAT** 0.
CARBOHYDRATE 22.45 g **FIBRE** 3.05 g
ADDED SUGAR 0.96 g **SALT** 0.24 g

1 Halve the melon and remove the seeds with a teaspoon. With a melon baller, carefully scoop the flesh into balls.

2 With a sharp knife, peel the grapefruit and remove all the white pith. Remove the segments by cutting between the membranes, holding the fruit over a small bowl to catch any juices.

3 Whisk the mustard, vinegar, honey, chopped mint and grapefruit juices together in a mixing bowl. Add the melon balls together with the grapefruit and mix well. Chill for 30 minutes.

4 Ladle into four dishes and serve garnished with a sprig of fresh mint.

Creamy Cod Chowder

Serve this soup as a substantial starter or snack, or as a light main meal accompanied by warm crusty wholemeal bread.

NUTRITIONAL NOTES

PER PORTION:

ENERGY 200 Kcals / 840 KJ **PROTEIN** 24.71 g
FAT 1.23 g **SATURATED FAT** 0.32 g
CARBOHYDRATE 23.88 g **FIBRE** 0.85 g
ADDED SUGAR 2.44 g **SALT** 3.14 g

Serves 4–6

INGREDIENTS
350 g/12 oz smoked cod fillet
1 small onion, finely chopped
1 bay leaf
4 black peppercorns
900 ml/1½ pints/3¾ cups
   skimmed milk
10 ml/2 tsp cornflour
200 g/7 oz canned sweetcorn kernels
15 ml/1 tbsp chopped fresh parsley

parsley

milk

cornflour

bay leaf

onion

sweetcorn

cod fillet

1 Skin the fish with a knife and put into a large saucepan with the onion, bay leaf and peppercorns. Pour over the milk.

2 Bring to the boil. Reduce the heat and simmer very gently for 12-15 minutes, or until the fish is just cooked. Do not overcook.

3 Using a slotted spoon, lift out the fish and flake into large chunks. Remove the bay leaf and peppercorns and discard.

4 Blend the cornflour with 10 ml/2 tsp cold water and add to the saucepan. Bring to the boil and simmer for 1 minute or until slightly thickened.

5 Drain the sweetcorn kernels and add to the saucepan together with the flaked fish and parsley.

COOK'S TIP

The flavour of the chowder improves if made a day in advance. Chill in the refrigerator until required, then re-heat gently to prevent the fish from disintegrating.

6 Re-heat the soup until piping hot, but do not boil. Ladle into four or six soup bowls and serve straight away.

Devilled Onions en Croûte

Fill crisp bread cups with tender button onions tossed in a mustardy glaze.

Serves 4–6

INGREDIENTS
12 thin slices of white bread
225 g/8 oz baby button onions or
    shallots
150 ml/¼ pint/⅔ cup vegetable stock
15 ml/1 tbsp dry white wine or dry
    sherry
2 turkey rashers, cut into thin strips
10 ml/2 tsp Worcestershire sauce
5 ml/1 tsp tomato purée
¼ tsp prepared English mustard
salt and freshly ground black pepper
sprigs of flat-leaf parsley, to garnish

button onions

white bread

stock

parsley

turkey rashers

NUTRITIONAL NOTES
PER PORTION:

ENERGY 178 Kcals/749 KJ **PROTEIN** 9.42 g
FAT 1.57 g **SATURATED FAT** 0.30 g
CARBOHYDRATE 33.26 g **FIBRE** 1.82 g
ADDED SUGAR 0 **SALT** 1.23 g

1 Pre-heat the oven to 200°C/400°F/ Gas 6. Stamp out the bread into rounds with a 7.5cm/3in fluted biscuit cutter and use to line a twelve-cup patty tin.

2 Cover each bread case with non-stick baking paper, and fill with baking beans or rice. Bake 'blind' for 5 minutes in the pre-heated oven. Remove the paper and beans and continue to bake for a further 5 minutes, until lightly browned and crisp.

3 Meanwhile, put the button onions in a bowl and cover with boiling water. Leave for 3 minutes, then drain and rinse under cold water. Trim off their top and root ends and slip them out of their skins.

4 Simmer the onions and stock in a covered saucepan for 5 minutes. Uncover and cook, stirring occasionally until the stock has reduced entirely. Add all the remaining ingredients, except the flat-leaf parsley. Cook for 2-3 minutes. Fill the toast cups with the devilled onions. Serve hot, garnished with sprigs of flat-leaf parsley.

Guacamole with Crudités

This fresh-tasting spicy dip is made using peas instead of the traditional avocados.

Serves 4–6

INGREDIENTS

350 g/12 oz/2¼ cups frozen peas, defrosted
1 garlic clove, crushed
2 spring onions, trimmed and chopped
5 ml/1 tsp finely grated rind and juice of 1 lime
2.5 ml/½ tsp ground cumin
dash of Tabasco sauce
15 ml/1 tbsp reduced calorie mayonnaise
30 ml/2 tbsp chopped fresh coriander
salt and freshly ground black pepper
pinch of paprika and lime slices, to garnish

FOR THE CRUDITÉS

6 baby carrots
2 celery sticks
1 red-skinned eating apple
1 pear
15 ml/1 tbsp lemon or lime juice
6 baby sweetcorn

peas

vegetables

NUTRITIONAL NOTES

PER PORTION:

ENERGY 110 Kcals/460 KJ **PROTEIN** 6.22 g
FAT 2.29 g **SATURATED FAT** 0.49 g
CARBOHYDRATE 16.99 g **FIBRE** 6.73 g
ADDED SUGAR 0.21 g **SALT** 0.19 g

1 Put the peas, garlic clove, spring onions, lime rind and juice, cumin, Tabasco sauce, mayonnaise and salt and freshly ground black pepper into a food processor or a blender for a few minutes and process until smooth.

2 Add the chopped coriander and process for a few more seconds. Spoon into a serving bowl, cover with clear film and chill in the refrigerator for 30 minutes, to let the flavours develop.

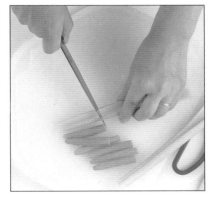

3 For the crudités, trim and peel the carrots. Halve the celery sticks lengthways and trim into sticks, the same length as the carrots. Quarter, core and thickly slice the apple and pear, then dip into the lemon or lime juice. Arrange with the baby sweetcorn on a platter.

4 Sprinkle the paprika over the guacamole and garnish with lime slices.

Crunchy Baked Mushrooms with Dill Dip

These crispy-coated bites are ideal as an informal starter or served with drinks.

NUTRITIONAL NOTES

Per portion:

ENERGY 173 Kcals/728 KJ | **PROTEIN** 11.88 g
FAT 6.04 g **SATURATED FAT** 3.24 g
CARBOHYDRATE 19.23 g **FIBRE** 1.99 g
ADDED SUGAR 0 **SALT** 0.91 g

Serves 4–6

INGREDIENTS
115 g/4 oz/2 cups fresh fine white
   breadcrumbs
15 g/½ oz/1½ tbsp finely grated
   mature Cheddar cheese
5 ml/1 tsp paprika
225 g/8 oz button mushrooms
2 egg whites

FOR THE TOMATO AND DILL DIP
4 ripe tomatoes
115 g/4 oz/½ cup curd cheese
60 ml/4 tbsp natural low fat yogurt
1 garlic clove, crushed
30 ml/2 tbsp chopped fresh dill
salt and freshly ground black pepper
sprig of fresh dill, to garnish

paprika

mushrooms

dill

tomatoes

breadcrumbs

curd cheese

1 Pre-heat the oven to 190°C/375°F/Gas 5. Mix together the breadcrumbs, cheese and paprika in a bowl.

2 Wipe the mushrooms clean and trim the stalks, if necessary. Lightly whisk the egg whites with a fork, until frothy.

3 Dip each mushroom into the egg whites, then into the breadcrumb mixture. Repeat until all the mushrooms are coated.

4 Put the mushrooms on a non-stick baking sheet. Bake in the pre-heated oven for 15 minutes, or until tender and the coating has turned golden and crunchy.

5 Meanwhile, to make the dip, plunge the tomatoes into a saucepan of boiling water for 1 minute, then into a saucepan of cold water. Slip off the skins. Halve, remove the seeds and cores and roughly chop the flesh.

6 Put the curd cheese, yogurt, garlic clove and dill into a mixing bowl and combine well. Season to taste. Stir in the chopped tomatoes. Spoon the mixture into a serving dish and garnish with a sprig of fresh dill. Serve the mushrooms hot, together with the dip.

Herby Fishcakes with Lemon and Chive Sauce

The wonderful flavour of fresh herbs makes these fishcakes the catch of the day.

Serves 4

INGREDIENTS
350 g/12 oz potatoes, peeled
75 ml/5 tbsp skimmed milk
350 g/12 oz haddock or hoki fillets, skinned
15 ml/1 tbsp lemon juice
15 ml/1 tbsp creamed horseradish sauce
30 ml/2 tbsp chopped fresh parsley
flour, for dusting
115 g/4 oz/2 cups fresh wholemeal breadcrumbs
salt and freshly ground black pepper
sprig of flat-leaf parsley, to garnish
mange tout and a sliced tomato and onion salad, to serve

FOR THE LEMON AND CHIVE SAUCE
thinly pared rind and juice of ½ small lemon
120 ml/4 fl oz/½ cup dry white wine
2 thin slices fresh root ginger
10 ml/2 tsp cornflour
30 ml/2 tbsp snipped fresh chives

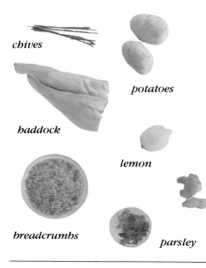

chives

potatoes

haddock

lemon

breadcrumbs

parsley

ginger

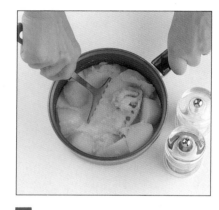

1 Cook the potatoes in a large saucepan of boiling water for 15-20 minutes. Drain and mash with the milk and season to taste.

2 Purée the fish together with the lemon juice and horseradish sauce in a blender or food processor. Mix together with the potatoes and parsley.

3 With floured hands, shape the mixture into eight fishcakes and coat with the breadcrumbs. Chill in the refrigerator for 30 minutes.

4 Cook the fishcakes under a pre-heated moderate grill for 5 minutes on each side, until browned.

5 To make the sauce, cut the lemon rind into julienne strips and put into a large saucepan together with the lemon juice, wine and ginger and season to taste.

NUTRITIONAL NOTES

PER PORTION:

ENERGY 232 Kcals / 975 KJ **PROTEIN** 19.99 g
FAT 1.99 g **SATURATED FAT** 0.26 g
CARBOHYDRATE 30.62 g **FIBRE** 3.11 g
ADDED SUGAR 0 **SALT** 0.82 g

6 Simmer uncovered for 6 minutes. Blend the cornflour with 15 ml/1 tbsp of cold water. Add to the saucepan and simmer until clear. Stir in the chives immediately before serving. Serve the sauce hot with the fishcakes, garnished with sprigs of flat-leaf parsley and accompanied with mange tout and a sliced tomato and onion salad.

Cajun-style Cod

This recipe works equally well with any firm-fleshed fish such as swordfish, shark, tuna or halibut.

Serves 4

INGREDIENTS
4 cod steaks, each weighing about
    175 g/6 oz
30 ml/2 tbsp natural low fat yogurt
15 ml/1 tbsp lime or lemon juice
1 garlic clove, crushed
5 ml/1 tsp ground cumin
5 ml/1 tsp paprika
5 ml/1 tsp mustard powder
2.5 ml/½ tsp cayenne pepper
2.5 ml/½ tsp dried thyme
2.5 ml/½ tsp dried oregano
new potatoes and a mixed salad,
    to serve

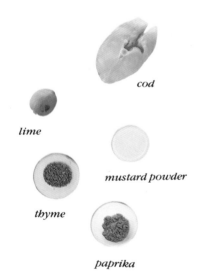

cod

lime

mustard powder

thyme

paprika

NUTRITIONAL NOTES

PER PORTION:

ENERGY 137 Kcals/577 KJ **PROTEIN** 28.42 g
FAT 1.75 g **SATURATED FAT** 0.26 g
CARBOHYDRATE 1.98 g **FIBRE** 0.06 g
ADDED SUGAR 0 **SALT** 0.32 g

1 Pat the fish dry on absorbent kitchen paper. Mix together the yogurt and lime or lemon juice and brush lightly over both sides of the fish.

2 Mix together the garlic clove, spices and herbs. Coat both sides of the fish with the seasoning mix, rubbing in well.

COOK'S TIP

If you don't have a ridged grill pan, heat several metal skewers under a grill until red hot. Holding the ends with a cloth, press onto the seasoned fish before cooking to give a ridged appearance.

3 Spray a ridged grill pan or heavy-based frying pan with non-stick cooking spray. Heat until very hot. Add the fish and cook over a high heat for 4 minutes, or until the underside is well browned.

4 Turn over and cook for a further 4 minutes, or until the steaks have cooked through. Serve immediately accompanied with new potatoes and a mixed salad.

Plaice Provençal

Re-create the taste of the Mediterranean with this easy-to-make fish casserole.

Serves 4

INGREDIENTS
4 large plaice fillets
2 small red onions
120 ml/4 fl oz/½ cup vegetable stock
60 ml/4 tbsp dry red wine
1 garlic clove, crushed
2 courgettes, sliced
1 yellow pepper, seeded and sliced
400 g/14 oz can chopped tomatoes
15 ml/1 tbsp chopped fresh thyme
salt and freshly ground black pepper
Potato Gratin, to serve

chopped tomatoes

plaice

thyme

courgettes

red onion   *pepper*

NUTRITIONAL NOTES
Per portion:

ENERGY 191 Kcals/802 KJ **PROTEIN** 29.46 g
FAT 3.77 g **SATURATED FAT** 0.61 g
CARBOHYDRATE 8.00 g **FIBRE** 1.97 g
ADDED SUGAR 0 **SALT** 0.57 g

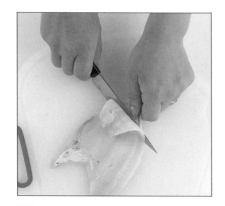

1 Pre-heat the oven to 180°C/350°F/Gas 4. Skin the plaice with a sharp knife by laying it skin-side down. Holding the tail end, push the knife between the skin and flesh in a sawing movement. Hold the knife at a slight angle with the blade towards the skin.

2 Cut each onion into eight wedges. Put into a heavy-based saucepan with the stock. Cover and simmer for 5 minutes. Uncover and continue to cook, stirring occasionally, until the stock has reduced entirely. Add the wine and garlic clove to the pan and continue to cook until the onions are soft.

3 Add the courgettes, yellow pepper, tomatoes and thyme and season to taste. Simmer for 3 minutes. Spoon the sauce into a large casserole.

4 Fold each fillet in half and place on top of the sauce. Cover and cook in the pre-heated oven for 15-20 minutes until the fish is opaque and cooked. Serve with Potato Gratin.

Seafood Pasta Shells with Spinach Sauce

You'll need very large pasta shells, measuring about 4 cm/1½ in long for this dish; don't try stuffing smaller shells – they're much too fiddly!

NUTRITIONAL NOTES
Per portion:

ENERGY 399 Kcals / 1676 KJ **PROTEIN** 32.69 g
FAT 12.79 g **SATURATED FAT** 5.81 g
CARBOHYDRATE 40.75 g **FIBRE** 3.31 g
ADDED SUGAR 0 **SALT** 3.59 g

Serves 4

INGREDIENTS
15 g/½ oz/1 tbsp low fat spread
8 spring onions, finely sliced
6 tomatoes
32 large dried pasta shells
225 g/8 oz/1 cup low fat soft cheese
90 ml/6 tbsp skimmed milk
pinch of freshly grated nutmeg
225 g/8 oz prawns
175 g/6 oz can white crabmeat,
   drained and flaked
115 g/4 oz frozen chopped spinach,
   thawed and drained
salt and freshly ground black pepper

spring onions

prawns

pasta shells

crabmeat

spinach

tomatoes

1 Pre-heat the oven to 150°C/300°F/ Gas 2. Melt the low fat spread in a small saucepan and gently cook the spring onions for 3-4 minutes, or until softened.

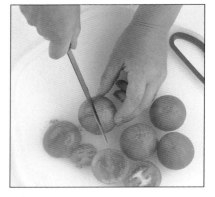

2 Plunge the tomatoes into a saucepan of boiling water for 1 minute, then into a saucepan of cold water. Slip off the skins. Halve the tomatoes, remove the seeds and cores and roughly chop the flesh.

3 Cook the pasta shells in lightly salted boiling water for about 10 minutes, or until *al dente*. Drain well.

4 Put the low fat soft cheese and skimmed milk into a saucepan and heat gently, stirring until blended. Season with salt, freshly ground black pepper and a pinch of nutmeg. Measure 30 ml/2 tbsp of the sauce into a bowl.

5 Add the spring onions, tomatoes, prawns, and crabmeat to the bowl. Mix well. Spoon the filling into the shells and place in a single layer in a shallow ovenproof dish. Cover with foil and cook in the pre-heated oven for 10 minutes.

6 Stir the spinach into the remaining sauce. Bring to the boil and simmer gently for 1 minute, stirring all the time. Drizzle over the pasta shells and serve hot.

Turkey Tonnato

This low fat version of the Italian dish 'vitello tonnato' is garnished with fine strips of red pepper instead of the traditional anchovy fillets.

NUTRITIONAL NOTES

Per portion:

ENERGY 235 Kcals / 988 KJ PROTEIN 35.47 g
FAT 7.09 g SATURATED FAT 1.33 g
CARBOHYDRATE 7.80 g FIBRE 1.37 g
ADDED SUGAR 1.04 g SALT 0.87 g

Serves 4

INGREDIENTS
450 g/1 lb turkey fillets
1 small onion, sliced
1 bay leaf
4 black peppercorns
350 ml/12 fl oz/1½ cups
   chicken stock
200 g/7 oz can tuna in brine, drained
75 ml/5 tbsp reduced calorie
   mayonnaise
30 ml/2 tbsp lemon juice
2 red peppers, seeded and
   thinly sliced
about 25 capers, drained
pinch of salt
mixed salad and tomatoes, to serve

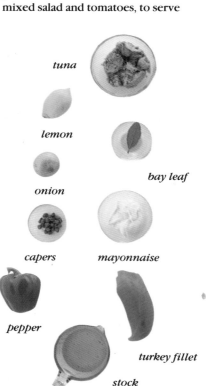

tuna

lemon

onion

bay leaf

capers

mayonnaise

pepper

turkey fillet

stock

1 Put the turkey fillets in a single layer in a large, heavy-based saucepan. Add the onion, bay leaf, peppercorns and stock. Bring to the boil and reduce the heat. Cover and simmer for 12 minutes, or until tender.

2 Turn off the heat and leave the turkey to cool in the stock, then remove with a slotted spoon. Slice thickly and arrange on a serving plate.

3 Boil the stock until reduced to about 75 ml/5 tbsp. Strain and leave to cool.

4 Put the tuna, mayonnaise, lemon juice, 45 ml/3 tbsp of the reduced stock and salt into a blender or food processor and purée until smooth.

5 Stir in enough of the remaining stock to reduce the sauce to the thickness of double cream. Spoon over the turkey.

6 Arrange the strips of red pepper in a lattice pattern over the turkey. Put a caper in the centre of each square. Chill in the refrigerator for 1 hour and serve with a fresh mixed salad and tomatoes.

NUTRITIONAL NOTES

Per portion:

ENERGY 320 Kcals / 1342 KJ **PROTEIN** 40.27 g
FAT 8.81 g **SATURATED FAT** 1.72 g
CARBOHYDRATE 21.17 g **FIBRE** 0.97 g
ADDED SUGAR 0 **SALT** 1.11 g

6 Put the chicken on a non-stick baking sheet and spray with non-stick cooking spray. Bake in the pre-heated oven for 25 minutes or until the coating is golden brown and the chicken completely cooked. Remove the cocktail sticks and serve with duchesse potatoes, French beans and grilled tomatoes.

Hot and Sour Pork

Chinese five-spice powder is made from a mixture of ground star anise, Szechuan pepper, cassia, cloves and fennel seed and has a flavour similar to liquorice. If you can't find any, use mixed spice instead.

NUTRITIONAL NOTES

PER PORTION:

ENERGY 196 K Cals/823 KJ **PROTEIN** 19.78 g
FAT 7.29 g **SATURATED FAT** 2.37 g
CARBOHYDRATE 13.63 g **FIBRE** 1.16 g
ADDED SUGAR 0 **SALT** 0.77 g

Serves 4

INGREDIENTS

350 g/12 oz pork fillet
5 ml/1 tsp sunflower oil
2.5 cm/1 in piece root ginger, grated
1 red chilli, seeded and finely
    chopped
5 ml/1 tsp Chinese five-spice powder
15 ml/1 tbsp sherry vinegar
15 ml/1 tbsp soy sauce
225 g/8 oz can pineapple chunks in
    natural juice
175 ml/6 fl oz/¾ cup chicken stock
20 ml/4 tsp cornflour
1 small green pepper, seeded and
    sliced
115 g/4 oz baby sweetcorn, halved
salt and freshly ground black pepper
sprig of flat-leaf parsley, to garnish
boiled rice, to serve

pineapple chunks

pork fillet

chilli

cornflour

soy sauce

pepper

baby sweetcorn

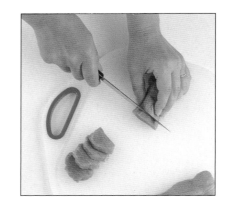

1 Pre-heat the oven to 160°C/325°F/ Gas 3. Trim away any visible fat from the pork and cut into 1 cm/½ in thick slices.

2 Brush the sunflower oil over the base of a flameproof casserole. Heat over a medium flame, then fry the meat for about 2 minutes on each side or until lightly browned.

3 Blend together the ginger, chilli, five-spice powder, vinegar and soy sauce.

4 Drain the pineapple chunks, reserving the juice. Make the stock up to 300 ml/½ pint/1¼ cups with the reserved juice, mix together with the spices and pour over the pork.

5 Slowly bring to the boil. Blend the cornflour with 15 ml/1 tbsp of cold water and gradually stir into the pork. Add the vegetables and season to taste.

6 Cover and cook in the oven for 30 minutes. Stir in the pineapple and cook for a further 5 minutes. Garnish with flat-leaf parsley and serve with boiled rice.

Honey-roast Pork with Thyme and Rosemary

Herbs and honey add flavour and sweetness to tenderloin – the leanest cut of pork.

Serves 4

INGREDIENTS
450 g/1 lb pork tenderloin
30 ml/2 tbsp thick honey
30 ml/2 tbsp Dijon mustard
5 ml/1 tsp chopped fresh rosemary
2.5 ml/½ tsp chopped fresh thyme
¼ tsp whole tropical peppercorns
sprigs of fresh rosemary and thyme, to garnish
Potato Gratin and cauliflower, to serve

FOR THE RED ONION CONFIT
4 red onions
350 ml/12 fl oz/1½ cups vegetable stock
15 ml/1 tbsp red wine vinegar
15 ml/1 tbsp caster sugar
1 garlic clove, crushed
30 ml/2 tbsp ruby port
pinch of salt

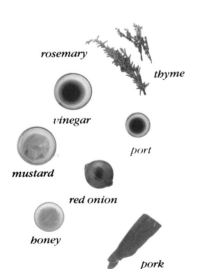

rosemary

thyme

vinegar

port

mustard

red onion

honey

pork

NUTRITIONAL NOTES
PER PORTION:

ENERGY 256 K Cals / 1078 KJ PROTEIN 25.01 g
FAT 8.92 g SATURATED FAT 2.92 g
CARBOHYDRATE 18.09 g FIBRE 1.10 g
ADDED SUGAR 10.57 g SALT 0.79 g

1 Pre-heat the oven to 180°C/350°F/Gas 4. Trim off any visible fat from the pork. Put the honey, mustard, rosemary and thyme in a small bowl and mix them together well.

2 Crush the peppercorns using a pestle and mortar. Spread the honey mixture over the pork and sprinkle with the crushed peppercorns. Place in a non-stick roasting tin and cook in the pre-heated oven for 35-45 minutes.

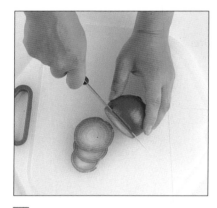

3 For the red onion confit, slice the onions into rings and put them into a heavy-based saucepan.

4 Add the stock, vinegar, sugar and garlic clove to the saucepan. Bring to the boil, then reduce the heat. Cover and simmer for 15 minutes.

5 Uncover and pour in the port and continue to simmer, stirring occasionally, until the onions are soft and the juices thick and syrupy. Season to taste with salt.

6 Cut the pork into slices and arrange on four warmed plates. Serve garnished with rosemary and thyme and accompanied with the red onion confit, Potato Gratin and cauliflower.

Tagliatelle with Sun-dried Tomatoes

Choose plain sun-dried tomatoes for this sauce, instead of those preserved in oil, as they will increase the fat content.

Serves 4

INGREDIENTS
1 garlic clove, crushed
1 celery stick, finely sliced
115 g/4 oz/1 cup sun-dried tomatoes, finely chopped
90 ml/3½ fl oz/scant ½ cup red wine
8 plum tomatoes
350 g/12 oz dried tagliatelle
salt and freshly ground black pepper

sun-dried tomatoes

celery

tagliatelle

plum tomatoes

NUTRITIONAL NOTES
PER PORTION:

ENERGY 357 K Cals/1499 KJ PROTEIN 12.36 g
FAT 2.32 g SATURATED FAT 0.32 g
CARBOHYDRATE 72.55 g FIBRE 5.09 g
ADDED SUGAR 0 SALT 0.09 g

1 Put the garlic, celery, sun-dried tomatoes and wine into a large saucepan. Gently cook for 15 minutes.

2 Plunge the plum tomatoes into a saucepan of boiling water for 1 minute, then into a saucepan of cold water. Slip off their skins. Halve, remove the seeds and cores and roughly chop the flesh.

3 Add the plum tomatoes to the saucepan and simmer for a further 5 minutes. Season to taste.

4 Meanwhile, cook the tagliatelle in plenty of lightly salted rapidly boiling water for 8-10 minutes, or until *al dente*. Drain well. Toss with half the sauce and serve on warmed plates, topped with the remaining sauce.

Chilli Bean Bake

The contrasting textures of saucy beans, vegetables and crunchy cornbread topping make this a memorable meal.

Serves 4

INGREDIENTS
225 g/8 oz/1⅓ cups red kidney beans
1 bay leaf
1 large onion, finely chopped
1 garlic clove, crushed
2 celery sticks, sliced
5 ml/1 tsp ground cumin
5 ml/1 tsp chilli powder
400 g/14 oz can chopped tomatoes
15 ml/1 tbsp tomato purée
5 ml/1 tsp dried mixed herbs
15 ml/1 tbsp lemon juice
1 yellow pepper, seeded and diced
salt and freshly ground black pepper
mixed salad, to serve

FOR THE CORNBREAD TOPPING
175 g/6 oz/1½ cups corn meal
15 ml/1 tbsp wholemeal flour
5 ml/1 tsp baking powder
1 egg, beaten
175 ml/6 fl oz/¾ cup skimmed milk

kidney beans

celery

tomato purée

pepper

NUTRITIONAL NOTES
PER PORTION:

ENERGY 399 K Cals/1675 KJ **PROTEIN** 22.86 g
FAT 4.65 g **SATURATED FAT** 0.86 g
CARBOHYDRATE 70.86 g **FIBRE** 11.59 g
ADDED SUGAR 0 **SALT** 0.72 g

1 Soak the beans overnight in cold water. Drain and rinse well. Pour 1 litre/1¾ pints/4 cups of water into a large, heavy-based saucepan together with the beans and bay leaf and boil rapidly for 10 minutes. Lower the heat, cover and simmer for 35–40 minutes, or until the beans are tender.

2 Add the onion, garlic clove, celery, cumin, chilli powder, chopped tomatoes, tomato purée and dried mixed herbs. Half-cover the pan with a lid and simmer for a further 10 minutes.

3 Stir in the lemon juice, yellow pepper and seasoning. Simmer for a further 8-10 minutes, stirring occasionally, until the vegetables are just tender. Discard the bay leaf and spoon the mixture into a large casserole.

4 Pre-heat the oven to 220°C/425°F/Gas 7. For the topping, put the corn meal, flour, baking powder and a pinch of salt into a bowl and mix together. Make a well in the centre and add the egg and milk. Mix and pour over the bean mixture. Bake in the pre-heated oven for 20 minutes, or until brown.

Ratatouille Pancakes

These pancakes are made slightly thicker than usual to hold the juicy vegetable filling.

Serves 4

INGREDIENTS
75 g/3 oz/¾ cup plain flour
25 g/1 oz/¼ cup medium oatmeal
1 egg
300 ml/½ pint/1¼ cups
   skimmed milk
mixed salad, to serve

FOR THE FILLING
1 large aubergine, cut into 2.5 cm/1 in
   cubes
1 garlic clove, crushed
2 medium courgettes, sliced
1 green pepper, seeded and sliced
1 red pepper, seeded and sliced
75 ml/5 tbsp vegetable stock
200 g/7 oz can chopped tomatoes
5 ml/1 tsp cornflour
salt and freshly ground black pepper

courgettes

oatmeal

pepper

cornflour

chopped tomatoes

aubergine

flour

egg

1 Sift the flour and a pinch of salt into a bowl. Stir in the oatmeal. Make a well in the centre, add the egg and half the milk and mix to a smooth batter. Gradually beat in the remaining milk. Cover the bowl and leave to stand for 30 minutes.

2 Spray a 18 cm/7 in pancake pan or heavy-based frying pan with non-stick cooking spray. Heat the pan, then pour in just enough batter to cover the base of the pan thinly. Cook for 2-3 minutes, until the underside is golden brown. Flip over and cook for a further 1-2 minutes.

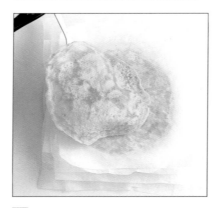

3 Slide the pancake out onto a plate lined with non-stick baking paper. Stack the other pancakes on top as they are made, interleaving each with non-stick baking paper. Keep warm.

4 For the filling, put the aubergine in a colander and sprinkle well with salt. Leave to stand on a plate for 30 minutes. Rinse thoroughly and drain well.

5 Put the garlic clove, courgettes, peppers, stock and tomatoes into a large saucepan. Simmer uncovered and stir occasionally for 10 minutes. Add the aubergine and cook for a further 15 minutes. Blend the cornflour with 10 ml/ 2 tsp water and add to the saucepan. Simmer for 2 minutes. Season to taste.

NUTRITIONAL NOTES

Per portion:

Energy 182 K Cals / 767 KJ **Protein** 9.36 g
Fat 3.07 g **Saturated Fat** 0.62 g
Carbohydrate 31.40 g **Fibre** 4.73 g
Added Sugar 0 **Salt** 0.22 g

6 Spoon the ratatouille mixture into the middle of each pancake. Fold each one in half, then in half again to make a cone shape. Serve hot with a mixed salad.

Vegetable Biryani

This exotic dish made from everyday ingredients will be appreciated by vegetarians and meat eaters alike.

Serves 4–6

NUTRITIONAL NOTES

PER PORTION:

ENERGY 175 K Cals/737 KJ **PROTEIN** 3.66 g
FAT 0.78 g **SATURATED FAT** 0.12 g
CARBOHYDRATE 41.03 g **FIBRE** 0.58 g
ADDED SUGAR 0 **SALT** 0.02 g

INGREDIENTS

175 g/6 oz/1 cup long-grain rice
2 whole cloves
seeds of 2 cardamom pods
450 ml/¾ pint/scant 2 cups
    vegetable stock
2 garlic cloves
1 small onion, roughly chopped
5 ml/1 tsp cumin seeds
5 ml/1 tsp ground coriander
2.5 ml/½ tsp ground turmeric
2.5 ml/½ tsp chilli powder
1 large potato, peeled and cut into
    2.5 cm/1 in cubes
2 carrots, sliced
½ cauliflower, broken into florets
50 g/2 oz French beans, cut into
    2.5 cm/1 in lengths
30 ml/2 tbsp chopped fresh coriander
30 ml/2 tbsp lime juice
salt and freshly ground black pepper
sprig of fresh coriander, to garnish

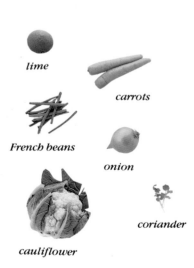

lime

carrots

French beans

onion

cauliflower

coriander

1 Put the rice, cloves and cardamom seeds into a large, heavy-based saucepan. Pour over the stock and bring to the boil.

2 Reduce the heat, cover and simmer for 20 minutes, or until all the stock has been absorbed.

3 Meanwhile put the garlic cloves, onion, cumin seeds, coriander, turmeric, chilli powder and seasoning into a blender or coffee grinder together with 30 ml/ 2 tbsp water. Blend to a paste.

4 Preheat the oven to 180°C/350°F/ Gas 4. Spoon the spicy paste into a flameproof casserole and cook over a low heat for 2 minutes, stirring occasionally.

5 Add the potato, carrots, cauliflower, beans and 90 ml/6 tbsp water. Cover and cook over a low heat for a further 12 minutes, stirring occasionally. Add the chopped coriander.

6 Spoon the rice over the vegetables. Sprinkle over the lime juice. Cover and cook in the oven for 25 minutes, or until the vegetables are tender. Fluff up the rice with a fork before serving and garnish with a sprig of fresh coriander.

Herby Baked Tomatoes

Dress up sliced, sweet tomatoes with fresh herbs and a crisp breadcrumb topping.

Serves 4–6

INGREDIENTS

675 g/1½ lb (about 8) large red and
   yellow tomatoes
10 ml/2 tsp red wine vinegar
2.5 ml/½ tsp wholegrain mustard
1 garlic clove, crushed
10 ml/2 tsp chopped fresh parsley
10 ml/2 tsp snipped fresh chives
25 g/1 oz/½ cup fresh fine white
   breadcrumbs
salt and freshly ground black pepper
sprigs of flat-leaf parsley, to garnish

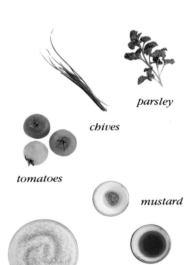

parsley

chives

tomatoes

mustard

vinegar

breadcrumbs

NUTRITIONAL NOTES
PER PORTION:

ENERGY 47 K Cals/196 KJ **PROTEIN** 1.97 g
FAT 0.73 g **SATURATED FAT** 0.08 g
CARBOHYDRATE 8.63 g **FIBRE** 1.98 g
ADDED SUGAR 0 **SALT** 0.15 g

1 Pre-heat the oven to 200°C/400°F/ Gas 6. Thickly slice the tomatoes and arrange half of them in a 900 ml/ 1½ pint/3¾ cup ovenproof dish.

2 Mix the vinegar, mustard, garlic clove and seasoning together. Stir in 10 ml/2 tsp of cold water. Sprinkle the tomatoes with half the parsley and chives, then drizzle over half the dressing.

3 Lay the remaining tomato slices on top, overlapping them slightly. Drizzle with the remaining dressing.

4 Sprinkle over the breadcrumbs. Bake in the pre-heated oven for 25 minutes or until the topping is golden. Sprinkle with the remaining parsley and chives. Serve immediately garnished with sprigs of flat-leaf parsley.

Courgettes in Citrus Sauce

If baby courgettes are unavailable, you can use larger ones, but they should be cooked whole so that they don't absorb too much water. Halve them lengthways and cut into 10 cm/4 in lengths.

Serves 4

INGREDIENTS
350 g/12 oz baby courgettes
4 spring onions, finely sliced
2.5 cm/1 in fresh root ginger, grated
30 ml/2 tbsp cider vinegar
15 ml/1 tbsp light soy sauce
5 ml/1 tsp soft light brown sugar
45 ml/3 tbsp vegetable stock
finely grated rind and juice of ½
    lemon and ½ orange
5 ml/1 tsp cornflour

orange

lemon

courgettes

ginger

spring onions

NUTRITIONAL NOTES
PER PORTION:

ENERGY 33 K Cals/138 KJ **PROTEIN** 2.18 g
FAT 0.42 g **SATURATED FAT** 0.09 g
CARBOHYDRATE 5.33 g **FIBRE** 0.92 g
ADDED SUGAR 1.31 g **SALT** 0.55 g

1 Cook the courgettes in lightly salted boiling water for 3-4 minutes, or until just tender. Drain well.

2 Meanwhile put all the remaining ingredients, except the cornflour, into a small saucepan and bring to the boil. Simmer for 3 minutes.

3 Blend the cornflour with 10 ml/2 tsp of cold water and add to the sauce. Bring to the boil, stirring continuously, until the sauce has thickened.

4 Pour the sauce over the courgettes and gently heat, shaking the pan to coat evenly. Transfer to a warmed serving dish and serve.

Mixed Mushroom Ragout

These mushrooms are delicious served hot or cold and can be made up to two days in advance.

Serves 4

NUTRITIONAL NOTES
PER PORTION:

ENERGY 41 K Cals / 172 KJ **PROTEIN** 2.51 g
FAT 0.66 g **SATURATED FAT** 0.08 g
CARBOHYDRATE 5.70 g **FIBRE** 1.02 g
ADDED SUGAR 2.64 g **SALT** 0.63 g

INGREDIENTS
1 small onion, finely chopped
1 garlic clove, crushed
5 ml/1 tsp coriander seeds, crushed
30 ml/2 tbsp red wine vinegar
15 ml/1 tbsp soy sauce
15 ml/1 tbsp dry sherry
10 ml/2 tsp tomato purée
10 ml/2 tsp soft light brown sugar
150 ml/¼ pint/⅔ cup vegetable stock
115 g/4 oz baby button mushrooms
115 g/4 oz chestnut mushrooms,
　quartered
115 g/4 oz oyster mushrooms, sliced
salt and freshly ground black pepper
sprig of fresh coriander, to garnish

oyster mushrooms

sherry

chestnut mushrooms

soy sauce

vinegar

coriander seeds

tomato purée

garlic

coriander

button mushrooms

onion

1 Put the first nine ingredients into a large saucepan. Bring to the boil and reduce the heat. Cover and simmer for 5 minutes.

2 Uncover the saucepan and simmer for 5 more minutes, or until the liquid has reduced by half.

3 Add the baby button and chestnut mushrooms and simmer for 3 minutes. Stir in the oyster mushrooms and cook for a further 2 minutes.

4 Remove the mushrooms with a slotted spoon and transfer them to a serving dish.

5 Boil the juices for about 5 minutes, or until reduced to about 75 ml/5 tbsp. Season to taste.

6 Allow to cool for 2-3 minutes, then pour over the mushrooms. Serve hot or well chilled, garnished with a sprig of fresh coriander.

Cracked Wheat and Mint Salad

Also known as bulgar wheat, burghul or pourgouri, cracked wheat has been partially cooked, so it requires only a short soaking before serving.

Serves 4

INGREDIENTS
250 g/9 oz/1⅔ cups cracked wheat
4 tomatoes
4 small courgettes, thinly sliced lengthways
4 spring onions, sliced on the diagonal
8 ready-to-eat dried apricots, chopped
40 g/1½ oz/¼ cup raisins
juice of 1 lemon
30 ml/2 tbsp tomato juice
45 ml/3 tbsp chopped fresh mint
1 garlic clove, crushed
salt and freshly ground black pepper
sprig of fresh mint, to garnish

courgettes

cracked wheat

tomatoes

lemon

spring onions

NUTRITIONAL NOTES
PER PORTION:

ENERGY 293 K Cals / 1231 KJ **PROTEIN** 8.72 g
FAT 1.69 g **SATURATED FAT** 0.28 g
CARBOHYDRATE 62.64 g **FIBRE** 2.25 g
ADDED SUGAR 0.24 g **SALT** 0.09 g

1 Put the cracked wheat into a large bowl. Add enough cold water to come 2.5 cm/1 in above the level of the wheat. Leave to soak for 30 minutes, then drain well and squeeze out any excess water in a clean dish towel.

2 Meanwhile plunge the tomatoes into boiling water for 1 minute and then into cold water. Slip off the skins. Halve, remove the seeds and cores and roughly chop the flesh.

3 Stir the chopped tomatoes, courgettes, spring onions, apricots, and raisins into the cracked wheat.

4 Put the lemon and tomato juice, mint, garlic clove and seasoning into a small bowl and whisk together with a fork. Pour over the salad and mix well. Chill in the refrigerator for at least 1 hour. Serve garnished with a sprig of mint.

Vegetables à la Greque

This simple side salad is made with winter vegetables, but you can vary it according to the season.

Serves 4

INGREDIENTS
175 ml/6 fl oz/¾ cup white wine
5 ml/1 tsp olive oil
30 ml/2 tbsp lemon juice
2 bay leaves
sprig of fresh thyme
4 juniper berries
450 g/1 lb leeks, trimmed and cut into
   2.5 cm/1 in lengths
1 small cauliflower, broken into
   florets
4 celery sticks, sliced on the diagonal
30 ml/2 tbsp chopped fresh parsley
salt and freshly ground black pepper

wine

celery

cauliflower

parsley

olive oil

leeks

NUTRITIONAL NOTES
Per portion:

ENERGY 88 K Cals / 368 KJ   **PROTEIN** 4.53 g
FAT 2.05 g   **SATURATED FAT** 0.11 g
CARBOHYDRATE 6.16 g   **FIBRE** 4.42 g
ADDED SUGAR 0   **SALT** 0.11 g

1 Put the wine, oil, lemon juice, bay leaves, thyme and juniper berries into a large, heavy-based saucepan and bring to the boil. Cover and leave to simmer for 20 minutes.

2 Add the leeks, cauliflower and celery. Simmer very gently for 5–6 minutes or until just tender.

COOK'S TIP
Choose a dry or medium-dry white wine for this dish.

3 Remove the vegetables with a slotted spoon and transfer them to a serving dish. Briskly boil the cooking liquid for 15-20 minutes, or until reduced by half. Strain.

4 Stir the parsley into the liquid and season to taste. Pour over the vegetables and leave to cool. Chill in the refrigerator for at least 1 hour before serving.

Fruit and Fibre Salad

Fresh, fast and filling, this salad makes a great starter, supper or snack.

Serves 4–6

INGREDIENTS
225 g/8 oz red or white cabbage or a mixture of both
3 medium carrots
1 pear
1 red-skinned eating apple
200 g/7 oz can green flageolet beans, drained
50 g/2 oz/¼ cup chopped dates

FOR THE DRESSING
2.5 ml/½ tsp dry English mustard
10 ml/2 tsp clear honey
30 ml/2 tbsp orange juice
5 ml/1 tsp white wine vinegar
2.5 ml/½ tsp paprika
salt and freshly ground black pepper

carrot

dates

orange

flageolet beans

cabbage   *pear*   *apple*

1 Shred the cabbage very finely, discarding any tough stalks.

2 Cut the carrots into very thin strips, about 5 cm/2 in long.

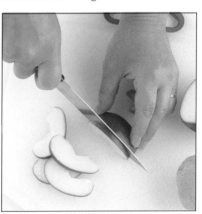

3 Quarter, core and slice the pear and apple, leaving the skin on.

4 Put the fruit and vegetables in a bowl with the beans and dates. Mix well.

5 For the dressing, blend the mustard with the honey until smooth. Add the orange juice, vinegar, paprika and seasoning and mix well.

NUTRITIONAL NOTES

PER PORTION:

ENERGY 137 K Cals / 574 KJ **PROTEIN** 4.56 g
FAT 0.87 g **SATURATED FAT** 0.03 g
CARBOHYDRATE 29.43 g **FIBRE** 6.28 g
ADDED SUGAR 1.91 g **SALT** 0.30 g

6 Pour the dressing over the salad and toss to coat. Chill in the refrigerator for 30 minutes before serving.

Potato Gratin

Don't rinse the potato slices before layering because the starch makes a thick sauce during cooking.

Serves 4

INGREDIENTS
1 garlic clove
5 large baking potatoes, peeled
45 ml/3 tbsp freshly grated Parmesan
  cheese
600 ml/1 pint/2½ cups vegetable or
  chicken stock
pinch of freshly grated nutmeg
salt and freshly ground black pepper

potatoes

Parmesan cheese

stock

NUTRITIONAL NOTES
PER PORTION:

ENERGY 221 K Cals/927 KJ **PROTEIN** 7.88 g
FAT 2.71 g **SATURATED FAT** 1.30 g
CARBOHYDRATE 43.77 g **FIBRE** 3.30 g
ADDED SUGAR 0 **SALT** 0.21 g

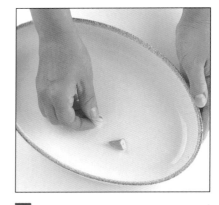

1 Pre-heat the oven to 200°C/400°F/ Gas 6. Halve the garlic clove and rub over the base and sides of a gratin dish measuring about 20 × 30 cm/8 × 12 in.

2 Slice the potatoes very thinly and arrange a third of them in the dish. Sprinkle with a little grated cheese, salt and freshly ground black pepper. Pour over some of the stock to prevent the potatoes from discolouring.

3 Continue layering the potatoes and cheese as before, then pour over the rest of the stock. Sprinkle with the grated nutmeg.

4 Bake in the oven for 1¼-1½ hours or until the potatoes are tender and the tops well browned.

VARIATION
For a potato and onion gratin, thinly slice one medium onion and layer with the potato.

Marinated Cucumber Salad

Sprinkling the cucumber with salt draws out some of the water and makes them crisper.

Serves 4–6

INGREDIENTS
2 medium cucumbers
15 ml/1 tbsp salt
90 g/3½ oz/½ cup granulated sugar
175 ml/6 fl oz/¾ cup dry cider
15 ml/1 tbsp cider vinegar
45 ml/3 tbsp chopped fresh dill
pinch of pepper

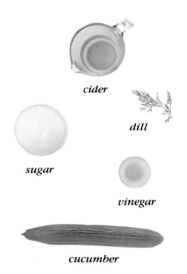

cider

dill

sugar

vinegar

cucumber

1 Slice the cucumbers thinly and place them in a colander, sprinkling salt between each layer. Put the colander over a bowl and leave to drain for 1 hour.

NUTRITIONAL NOTES
PER PORTION:

ENERGY 111 K Cals/465 KJ **PROTEIN** 0.52 g
FAT 0.14 g **SATURATED FAT** 0.01 g
CARBOHYDRATE 25.59 g **FIBRE** 0.62 g
ADDED SUGAR 23.62 g **SALT** 0.02 g

2 Thoroughly rinse the cucumber under cold running water to remove excess salt, then pat dry on absorbent kitchen paper.

3 Gently heat the sugar, cider and vinegar in a saucepan, until the sugar has dissolved. Remove from the heat and leave to cool. Put the cucumber slices in a bowl, pour over the cider mixture and leave to marinate for 2 hours.

4 Drain the cucumber and sprinkle with the dill and pepper to taste. Mix well and transfer to a serving dish. Chill in the refrigerator until ready to serve.

Apricot Delice

A fluffy mousse base with a layer of fruit jelly on top makes this dessert doubly delicious.

Serves 8

INGREDIENTS

2 × 400 g/14 oz cans apricots in natural juice
60 ml/4 tbsp fructose
15 ml/1 tbsp lemon juice
25 ml/5 tsp powdered gelatine
425 g/15 oz low fat ready-to-serve custard
150 ml/¼ pint/⅔ cup strained yogurt (see Introduction)
1 quantity yogurt piping cream (see Introduction), to decorate
1 apricot, sliced and sprig of fresh apple mint, to decorate

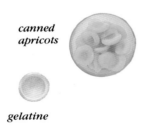

canned apricots

gelatine

custard

strained yogurt

apricots

NUTRITIONAL NOTES

PER PORTION:

ENERGY 155 K Cals/649 KJ **PROTEIN** 7.35 g
FAT 0.63 g **SATURATED FAT** 0.33 g
CARBOHYDRATE 31.89 g **FIBRE** 0.90 g
ADDED SUGAR 3.53 g **SALT** 0.26 g

1 Line the base of a 1.2 litre/2 pint/5 cup heart-shaped or round cake tin with non-stick baking paper.

2 Drain the apricots, reserving the juice. Put the drained apricots in a food processor or blender fitted with a metal blade together with the fructose and 60 ml/4 tbsp of the apricot juice. Blend to a smooth purée.

3 Measure 30 ml/2 tbsp of the apricot juice into a small bowl. Add the lemon juice, then sprinkle over 10 ml/2 tsp of the gelatine. Leave for about 5 minutes, until 'spongy'.

4 Stir the gelatine into half of the purée and pour into the prepared tin. Chill in a refrigerator for 1½ hours, or until firm.

COOK'S TIP

Don't use a loose-bottomed cake tin for this recipe as the mixture may seep through before it sets.

5 Sprinkle the remaining 15 ml/1 tbsp of gelatine over 60 ml/4 tbsp of the apricot juice. Soak and dissolve as before. Mix the remaining apricot purée with the custard, yogurt and gelatine. Pour onto the layer of set fruit purée and chill in the refrigerator for 3 hours.

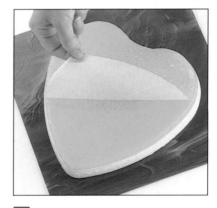

6 Dip the cake tin into hot water for a few seconds and unmould the delice onto a serving plate. Decorate with yogurt piping cream, the sliced apricot and sprigs of fresh apple mint.

Watermelon Sorbet

A slice of this refreshing sorbet is the perfect way to cool down on a hot sunny day.

Serves 4–6

INGREDIENTS
½ small watermelon, weighing about
   1 kg/2¼ lb
75 g/3 oz/½ cup caster sugar
60 ml/4 tbsp cranberry juice or water
30 ml/2 tbsp lemon juice
sprigs of fresh mint, to decorate

cranberry juice

sugar

watermelon *lemon juice*

NUTRITIONAL NOTES
PER PORTION:

ENERGY 125 K Cals / 525 K J **PROTEIN** 0.79 g
FAT 0.52 g **SATURATED FAT** 0
CARBOHYDRATE 31.29 g **FIBRE** 0.26 g
ADDED SUGAR 19.69 g **SALT** 0.01 g

1 Cut the watermelon into 4–6 equal-sized wedges (depending on the number of servings you require). Scoop out the pink flesh, discarding the seeds but reserving the shell.

2 Line a freezer-proof bowl, about the same size as the melon, with clear film. Arrange the melon skins in the bowl to re-form the shell, fitting them together snugly so that there are no gaps. Put in the freezer.

3 Put the sugar and cranberry juice or water in a saucepan and stir over a low heat until the sugar dissolves. Bring to the boil and simmer for 5 minutes. Leave the sugar syrup to cool.

4 Put the melon flesh and lemon juice in a blender and process to a smooth purée. Stir in the sugar syrup and pour into a freezer-proof container. Freeze for 3–3½ hours, or until slushy.

5 Tip the sorbet into a chilled bowl and whisk to break up the ice crystals. Return to the freezer for another 30 minutes, whisk again, then tip into the melon shell and freeze until solid.

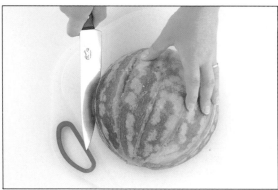

6 Remove from the freezer and leave to defrost at room temperature for 15 minutes. Take the melon out of the bowl and cut into wedges with a warmed sharp knife. Serve with sprigs of fresh mint.

COOK'S TIP

If preferred, this pretty pink sorbet can be served scooped into balls. Do this before the mixture is completely frozen and re-freeze the balls on a baking sheet, ready to serve.

Feather-light Peach Pudding

On chilly days, try this hot fruit pudding with its tantalizing sponge topping.

Serves 4

INGREDIENTS
400 g/14 oz can peach slices in
    natural juice
50 g/2 oz/4 tbsp low fat spread
40 g/1½ oz/¼ cup soft light
    brown sugar
1 egg, beaten
65 g/2½ oz/½ cup plain
    wholemeal flour
50 g/2 oz/½ cup plain flour
5 ml/1 tsp baking powder
2.5 ml/½ tsp ground cinnamon
60 ml/4 tbsp skimmed milk
2.5 ml/½ tsp vanilla essence
10 ml/2 tsp icing sugar, for dusting
low fat ready-to-serve custard,
    to serve

peach slices

flour

icing sugar

egg

brown sugar

low fat custard

NUTRITIONAL NOTES
PER PORTION:

ENERGY 255 K Cals / 1071 KJ **PROTEIN** 6.49 g
FAT 6.78 g **SATURATED FAT** 1.57 g
CARBOHYDRATE 44.70 g **FIBRE** 2.65 g
ADDED SUGAR 13.34 g **SALT** 0.70 g

1 Pre-heat the oven to 180°C/350°F/ Gas 4. Drain the peaches and put into a 1 litre/1¾ pint/4 cup pie dish with 30 ml/ 2 tbsp of the juice.

2 Put all the remaining ingredients, except the icing sugar into a mixing bowl. Beat for 3–4 minutes, until thoroughly combined.

COOK'S TIP
For a simple sauce, blend 5 ml/1 tsp arrowroot with 15 ml/1 tbsp peach juice in a small saucepan. Stir in the remaining peach juice from the can and bring to the boil. Simmer for 1 minute until thickened and clear.

3 Spoon the sponge mixture over the peaches and level the top evenly. Cook in the oven for 35-40 minutes, or until springy to the touch.

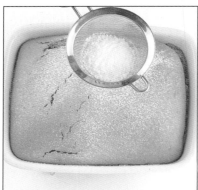

4 Lightly dust the top with icing sugar before serving hot with the custard.

Plum, Rum and Raisin Brulée

Crack through the crunchy caramel to find the juicy plums and smooth creamy centre of this dessert.

Serves 4

INGREDIENTS
25 g/1 oz/3 tbsp raisins
15 ml/1 tbsp dark rum
350 g/12 oz medium plums (about 6)
juice of 1 orange
15 ml/1 tbsp clear honey
225 g/8 oz/2 cups low fat soft cheese
90 g/3½ oz/½ cup granulated sugar

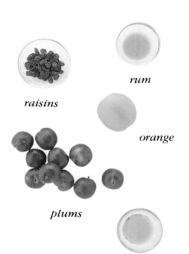

raisins

rum

orange

plums

honey

NUTRITIONAL NOTES

PER PORTION:

ENERGY 264 K Cals / 1110 KJ PROTEIN 5.71 g
FAT 8.56 g SATURATED FAT 5.11 g
CARBOHYDRATE 41.43 g FIBRE 1.45 g
ADDED SUGAR 26.49 g SALT 0.66 g

I Put the raisins into a small bowl and sprinkle over the rum. Leave to soak for 5 minutes.

2 Quarter the plums and remove their stones. Put into a large, heavy-based saucepan together with the orange juice and honey. Simmer gently for 5 minutes or until soft. Stir in the soaked raisins. Reserve 15 ml/1 tbsp of the juice, then divide the rest between four 150 ml/¼ pint/⅔ cup ramekin dishes.

3 Blend the low fat soft cheese with the reserved 15 ml/1 tbsp of plum juice. Spoon over the plums and chill in the refrigerator for 1 hour.

4 Put the sugar into a large, heavy-based saucepan with 45 ml/3 tbsp cold water. Heat gently, stirring, until the sugar has dissolved. Boil for 15 minutes or until it turns golden brown. Cool for 2 minutes, then carefully pour over the ramekins. Cool and serve.

Red Fruit Fool

Frozen soft fruit is available in most supermarkets, making this a year-round treat.

Serves 4

INGREDIENTS
450 g/1 lb mixed red fruit, such as
  raspberries, redcurrants and
  strawberries
10 ml/2 tsp fructose
2.5 ml/½ tsp arrowroot
150 ml/¼ pint/⅔ cup half fat
  whipping cream
5 ml/1 tsp vanilla essence
fresh fruit, to decorate

strawberries

redcurrants

raspberries

1 Put the fruit and fructose into a large heavy-based saucepan and simmer over a low heat for 2 minutes, or until just soft.

2 Blend the arrowroot with 10 ml/2 tsp cold water. Add to the fruit and simmer for a further minute, or until thickened. Cool and chill in the refrigerator for 1 hour.

3 Divide two-thirds of the fruit mixture between four individual glasses.

4 Purée the rest of the fruit and strain through a fine sieve to remove the pips.

5 Lightly whip the cream and vanilla essence together until soft peaks form. Fold in the remaining fruit purée.

6 Spoon the fruit cream mixture between the glasses and chill for 30 minutes. Serve decorated with fresh fruit.

NUTRITIONAL NOTES

PER PORTION:

ENERGY 105 K Cals/441 KJ **PROTEIN** 1.60 g
FAT 7.24 g **SATURATED FAT** 4.49 g
CARBOHYDRATE 8.88 g **FIBRE** 1.31 g
ADDED SUGAR 1.31 g **SALT** 0.05 g

COOK'S TIP

Fructose is a natural fruit sugar. It is slightly sweeter than granulated sugar (sucrose) so less is needed. If you use granulated sugar instead, use 15 ml/ 1 tbsp for this recipe.

Blushing Pears

Pears poached in rosé wine and sweet spices absorb all the subtle flavours and turn a soft pink colour.

Serves 6

INGREDIENTS
6 firm eating pears
300 ml/½ pint/1¼ cups rosé wine
150 ml/¼ pint/⅔ cup cranberry or
    clear apple juice
strip of thinly pared orange rind
1 cinnamon stick
4 whole cloves
1 bay leaf
75 ml/5 tbsp caster sugar
small bay leaves, to decorate

wine

pears   *cranberry juice*

cinnamon

sugar

orange

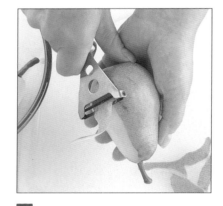

1 Thinly peel the pears with a sharp knife or vegetable peeler, leaving the stalks attached.

2 Pour the wine and cranberry or apple juice into a large heavy-based saucepan. Add the orange rind, cinnamon stick, cloves, bay leaf and sugar.

3 Heat gently, stirring all the time until the sugar has dissolved. Add the pears and stand them upright in the pan. Pour in enough cold water to barely cover them. Cover and cook very gently for 20–30 minutes, or until just tender, turning and basting occasionally.

4 Using a slotted spoon, gently lift the pears out of the syrup and transfer to a serving dish.

5 Bring the syrup to the boil and boil rapidly for 10–15 minutes, or until it has reduced by half.

COOK'S TIP

Check the pears by piercing with a skewer or sharp knife towards the end of the poaching time because some may cook more quickly than others.

NUTRITIONAL NOTES

Per portion:

ENERGY 148 K Cals/620 KJ **PROTEIN** 0.48 g
FAT 0.16 g **SATURATED FAT** 0
CARBOHYDRATE 30.18 g **FIBRE** 2.93 g
ADDED SUGAR 13.13 g **SALT** 0.02 g

6 Strain the syrup and pour over the pears. Serve hot or well-chilled, decorated with bay leaves.

Chocolate and Banana Brownies

Nuts traditionally give brownies their chewy texture. Here oat bran is used instead, creating a moist, morish, yet healthy alternative.

Makes 9

INGREDIENTS

75 ml/5 tbsp fat reduced cocoa powder
15 ml/1 tbsp caster sugar
75 ml/5 tbsp skimmed milk
3 large bananas, mashed
215 g/7½ oz/1 cup soft light brown sugar
5 ml/1 tsp vanilla essence
5 egg whites
75 g/3 oz/¾ cup self-raising flour
75 g/3 oz/¾ cup oat bran
15 ml/1 tbsp icing sugar, for dusting

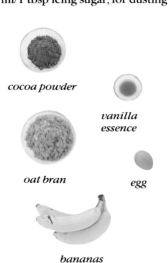

cocoa powder

vanilla essence

oat bran

egg

bananas

NUTRITIONAL NOTES

PER PORTION:

ENERGY 230 K Cals / 968 KJ **PROTEIN** 5.24 g
FAT 2.15 g **SATURATED FAT** 0.91 g
CARBOHYDRATE 50.74 g **FIBRE** 1.89 g
ADDED SUGAR 28.81 g **SALT** 0.32 g

1 Pre-heat the oven to 180°C/350°F/ Gas 4. Line a 20 cm/8 in square tin with non-stick baking paper.

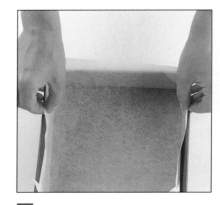

2 Blend the fat reduced cocoa powder and caster sugar with the skimmed milk. Add the bananas, soft brown sugar and vanilla essence.

COOK'S TIP

Store these brownies in an airtight tin for a day before eating – they improve with keeping.

3 Lightly beat the egg whites with a fork. Add the chocolate mixture and continue to beat well. Sift the flour over the mixture and fold in with the oat bran. Pour into the prepared tin.

4 Cook in the pre-heated oven for 40 minutes or until firm. Cool in the tin for 10 minutes, then turn out onto a wire rack. Cut into squares and lightly dust with icing sugar before serving.

Cheese and Chive Scones

Feta cheese makes an excellent substitute for butter in these tangy savoury scones.

Makes 9

INGREDIENTS
115 g/4 oz/1 cup self-raising flour
150 g/5 oz/1 cup self-raising
 wholemeal flour
2.5 ml/½ tsp salt
75 g/3 oz feta cheese
15 ml/1 tbsp snipped fresh chives
150 ml/¼ pint/⅔ cup skimmed milk,
 plus extra for glazing
1.25 ml/¼ tsp cayenne pepper

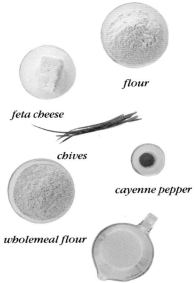

flour

feta cheese

chives

cayenne pepper

wholemeal flour

milk

NUTRITIONAL NOTES

PER PORTION:

ENERGY 121 K Cals / 507 KJ **PROTEIN** 5.15 g
FAT 2.24 g **SATURATED FAT** 1.13 g
CARBOHYDRATE 21.33 g **FIBRE** 1.92 g
ADDED SUGAR 0 **SALT** 0.72 g

1 Pre-heat the oven to 200°C/400°F/ Gas 6. Sift the flours and salt into a mixing bowl, adding any bran left over from the flour in the sieve.

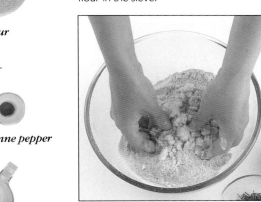

2 Crumble the feta cheese and rub into the dry ingredients. Stir in the chives, then add the milk and mix to a soft dough.

3 Turn out onto a floured surface and lightly knead until smooth. Roll out to 2 cm/¾ in thick and stamp out nine scones with a 6 cm/2½ in biscuit cutter.

4 Transfer the scones to a non-stick baking sheet. Brush with skimmed milk, then sprinkle over the cayenne pepper. Bake in the oven for 15 minutes, or until golden brown. Serve warm or cold.

Carrot and Courgette Cake

If you can't resist the lure of a slice of iced cake, you'll love this moist, spiced sponge with its delicious creamy topping.

NUTRITIONAL NOTES

Per portion:

ENERGY 173 K Cals / 728 KJ **PROTEIN** 6.25 g
FAT 6.31 g **SATURATED FAT** 2.22 g
CARBOHYDRATE 24.36 g **FIBRE** 1.84 g
ADDED SUGAR 12.92 g **SALT** 0.26 g

Serves 10

INGREDIENTS
1 medium carrot
1 medium courgette
3 eggs, separated
115 g/4 oz/scant ½ cup soft light
    brown sugar
30 ml/2 tbsp ground almonds
finely grated rind of 1 orange
150 g/5 oz/1 cup self-raising
    wholemeal flour
5 ml/1 tsp ground cinnamon
5 ml/1 tsp icing sugar, to dust
fondant carrots and courgettes, to
    decorate

FOR THE TOPPING
175 g/6 oz/¾ cup low fat soft cheese
5 ml/1 tsp clear honey

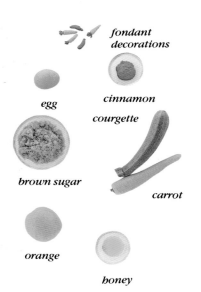

fondant decorations

egg

cinnamon

courgette

brown sugar

carrot

orange

honey

1 Pre-heat the oven to 180°C/350°F/ Gas 4. Line an 18 cm/7 in square tin with non-stick baking paper. Coarsely grate the carrot and courgette.

2 Put the egg yolks, sugar, ground almonds and orange rind into a bowl and whisk until very thick and light.

3 Sift together the flour and cinnamon and fold into the mixture together with the grated vegetables. Add any bran left over from the flour in the sieve.

4 Whisk the egg whites until stiff and carefully fold them in, a half at a time. Spoon into the prepared tin. Bake in the oven for 1 hour and cover the top with foil after 40 minutes.

5 Leave to cool in the tin for 5 minutes, then turn out onto a wire rack and carefully remove the lining paper.

6 For the topping, beat together the cheese and honey and spread over the cake. Decorate with fondant carrots and courgettes.

Chocolate and Orange Angel Cake

This light-as-air sponge with its fluffy icing is virtually fat free, yet tastes heavenly.

Serves 10

INGREDIENTS
25 g/1 oz/¼ cup plain flour
15 g/½ oz/2 tbsp fat reduced cocoa
    powder
15 g/½ oz/2 tbsp cornflour
pinch of salt
5 egg whites
2.5 ml/½ tsp cream of tartar
115 g/4 oz/scant ½ cup caster sugar
blanched and shredded rind of 1
    orange, to decorate

ICING
200 g/7 oz/1 cup caster sugar
1 egg white

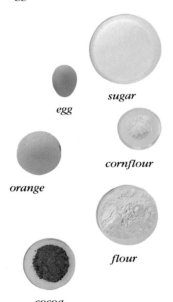

sugar

egg

cornflour

orange

flour

cocoa

1 Preheat the oven to 180°C/350°F/ Gas 4. Sift the flour, cocoa powder, cornflour and salt together three times. Beat the egg whites in a large bowl until foamy. Add the cream of tartar, then whisk until soft peaks form.

2 Add the caster sugar to the egg whites a spoonful at a time, whisking after each addition. Sift a third of the flour and cocoa mixture over the meringue and gently fold in. Repeat, sifting and folding in the flour and cocoa mixture two more times.

3 Spoon the mixture into a non-stick 20 cm/8 in ring mould and level the top. Bake in the oven for 35 minutes or until springy when lightly pressed. Turn upside-down onto a wire rack and leave to cool in the tin. Carefully ease out of the tin.

4 For the icing, put the sugar in a pan with 75 ml/5 tbsp cold water. Stir over a low heat until dissolved. Boil until the syrup reaches a temperature of 120°C/ 240°F on a sugar thermometer, or when a drop of the syrup makes a soft ball when dropped into a cup of cold water. Remove from the heat.

5 Whisk the egg white until stiff. Add the syrup in a thin stream, whisking all the time. Continue to whisk until the mixture is very thick and fluffy.

NUTRITIONAL NOTES

PER PORTION:

ENERGY 153 K Cals / 644 KJ **PROTEIN** 2.27 g
FAT 0.27 g **SATURATED FAT** 0.13 g
CARBOHYDRATE 37.79 g **FIBRE** 0.25 g
ADDED SUGAR 34.65 g **SALT** 0.25 g

COOK'S TIP

Make sure you do not over-beat the egg whites. They should not be stiff but should form soft peaks, so that the air bubbles can expand further during cooking and help the cake to rise.

6 Spread the icing over the top and sides of the cooled cake. Sprinkle the orange rind over the top of the cake and serve.

INDEX

USEFUL ADDRESSES

Lakeland Plastics Ltd.
Alexandra Buildings
Windermere
Cumbria. LA23 1BQ
(Mail order for heavy-gauge baking trays, non-stick coated fabric
sheets and measuring cups)

Parsons Trading Ltd.
P.O. Box 995
Purton
Swindon
Wilts. SN5 9WB
(Mail order for fat reduced cocoa)

ACKNOWLEDGEMENTS

The author and publishers would like to thank Wendy Doyle of the
Mother and Baby Clinic, London E9 for compiling the nutritional
information for each recipe.